ESSENTIAL TIPS

CACTI &
SUCCULENTS

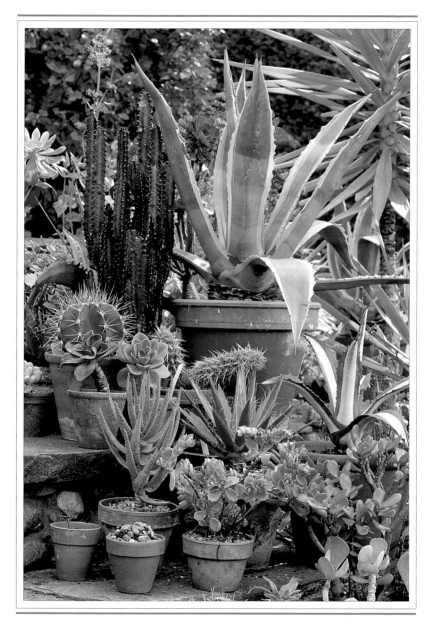

ESSENTIAL TIPS

CACTI &
SUCCULENTS

Terry Hewitt

DORLING KINDERSLEY
London • New York • Stuttgart • Moscow

A DORLING KINDERSLEY BOOK

Editor Bella Pringle
Art Editor Gill Della Casa
DTP Designer Mark Bracey
Series Editor Charlotte Davies
Series Art Editor Clive Hayball
Production Controller Lauren Britton

First published in Great Britain in 1996 by
Dorling Kindersley Limited,
9 Henrietta Street, London WC2E 8PS

Visit us on the World Wide Web at http://www.dk.com

A CIP catalogue record for this book is available from the British Library

ISBN 0-7513-0362-3

Text film output by The Right Type, Great Britain
Reproduced by Colourscan, Singapore
Printed and bound by Graphicom, Italy

ESSENTIAL TIPS

CACTI & SUCCULENT KNOW-HOW

1 WHAT ARE CACTI & SUCCULENT PLANTS?

The cacti family belongs to a larger group of plants known as succulents. All succulents have a specialized anatomy that enables them to survive drought or lack of light.

Succulents can store moisture in fleshy tissue in their stems, leaves, or roots, and many have developed features to reduce water loss. In adverse conditions, they can cease growing and remain dormant.

CROSS-SECTION

Water storage tissue

SIDE VIEW

◁ STEM SUCCULENTS
Plants that store large amounts of watery mucus in round or columnar stems. Water loss is kept to a minimum by their small surface area in proportion to volume. Nearly all cacti are stem succulents.

Spines reduce moisture loss

Tuberous roots store water

Fleshy leaves store water

Lower leaves help to shade soil and reduce evaporation

△ LEAF SUCCULENTS
Species with leaves that vary in size and form, depending on water availability. When water is present the leaves swell to become thick and fleshy but in drought they shrivel or are shed.

SIDE VIEW

CROSS-SECTION

Fleshy stem and leaves

② HOW CACTI DIFFER

Cacti are different from other succulents because they have areoles – pad-like buds – from which shoots, spines, and flowers grow. Only species of cacti have areoles, but take care when using this feature for identification as areoles are not always easy to see.

CLOSE-UP OF AREOLES ON SURFACE

◁ ROOT SUCCULENTS
Succulents that can store water underground in tuberous, or swollen roots. This feature enables these plants to survive long periods of drought. Below soil level, moisture loss occurs more slowly and there is less risk of damage by bush fire or grazing animals.

3 DO CACTI ONLY GROW IN DESERTS?

Although traditionally associated with arid desert and mountain landscapes, some cacti and other succulents inhabit tropical jungle. Here the climate is hot and humid and the plants have to contend with a lack of light rather than the usual lack of water. Some jungle cacti, such as *Epiphyllum* have flattened stems with a large surface area to absorb maximum light.

JUNGLE & DESERT HABITATS ▽ ▷
The success of cacti and other succulents partly depends on their ability to inhabit inhospitable jungle and desert areas where there is little competition from other plants.

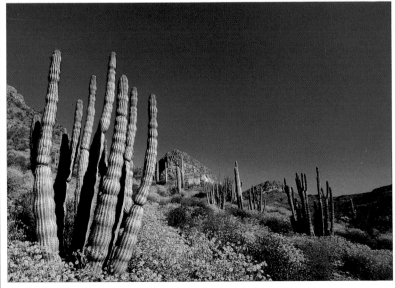

4 DO CACTI & SUCCULENTS NEED LESS CARE?

Many believe that because these plants grow in a hostile landscape they require little or no care when cultivated. They can tolerate some neglect and only a little water but, if forgotten, they will retreat into dormancy. Well cared for plants grow well and flower annually.

5 WHEN DO THEY FLOWER?

In arid desert regions, long, dry spells ensure cacti and succulents remain dormant for most of the year. To make up for this, many have developed a short life cycle. Once rain falls, they burst into active growth, producing leaves, flowers, and seeds in less than one month.

◁ DAY-FLOWERING CACTUS
Echinocereus triglochidiatus *produces a mass of bright red flowers that open fully in the summer sun.*

Flowers appear in summer when the plant reaches 1.2 m (4 ft) tall

Huge blooms grow directly from cactus stem

Petals open up to 25 cm (10 in) across

NIGHT-FLOWERING CACTUS
In summer, the flowers of Echinopsis scopulicola *open at dusk and close at dawn. The pale petals help moths locate them at night.*

6 WHERE TO BUY CACTI & SUCCULENTS

A huge variety of cacti and succulents can be cultivated but only a limited choice of species – usually those that are easy to grow – can be bought at garden centres or florists. Visit a specialist cactus nursery or local cactus show if you wish to buy a more unusual variety of plant.

Diseased leaves lack vigour

△ UNHEALTHY SUCCULENT

Mound of well-formed waxy leaves

Even growth of spines on plump stem

Uneven spine growth on limp, lop-sided stem

UNHEALTHY CACTUS ▷

BUYING HEALTHY PLANTS
When you have decided which variety of cactus or succulent to buy, the next step is to choose a healthy plant. Look for the tell-tale signs shown here and outlined below.

△ HEALTHY CACTUS

HEALTHY SUCCULENT △

7 HOW TO SELECT A HEALTHY CACTUS

The stem skin of a cactus reveals a great deal about the plant's health.
- Avoid plants with tired and dull stem skin or ones which have large, unsightly skin blemishes.
- Check that the spines are evenly distributed and are undamaged.
- Look at the compost in the pot. If it is fresh and weed-free the grower has cared for the plant.

8 SELECTING HEALTHY SUCCULENTS

Many succulents are leafy and by inspecting the leaves you can determine the plant's condition.
- Avoid succulents that have only a few leaves or have pale leaves, as this an obvious sign of poor growth.
- Examine the leaves present to make sure that none is deformed.
- Check that the level of compost in the pot has not dropped.

9 EASY CARE FOR BEGINNERS

Many of the species sold by florists and garden centres are ideal for beginners as they have often been selected on the basis that they are easy to care for. These cacti and succulents will tolerate some neglect and, unlike other species, they produce flowers when only a few years old.

△ PARODIA HERTERI

Pink flowers appear between spring and early autumn

Daisy-like flowers appear after two years

FAUCARIA TUBERCULOSA ▷

Triangular leaves tipped with "teeth"

▽ SEMPERVIVUM 'BELLOT'S POURPRE'

EASY CARE CACTI & SUCCULENTS
CACTI
Cereus aethiops
Ferocactus wislizeni
Gymnocalycium baldianum
Opuntia lindheimeri
Parodia herteri
Stenocactus multicostatus
SUCCULENTS
Adromischus cooperi
Cotyledon undulata
Echeveria elegans
Faucaria tuberculosa
Kalanchoe tomentosa
Sempervivum 'Bellot's Pourpre'
Senecio haworthii

13

DISPLAY & ARRANGEMENT

10 THE KEY TO A HEALTHY DISPLAY

Cacti and succulents are broadly divisible into desert plants which like dry sun, and jungle plants which prefer moist shade. When choosing a selection of plants to grow together, check that they have similar cultural needs, and bear in mind the final location for which they are intended. The more adept you are at matching the plants' needs to the limitations of the site, the more successful your plantings will be in the long term. For example, if you have a sunny spot on a window-sill select species that thrive in full sun.

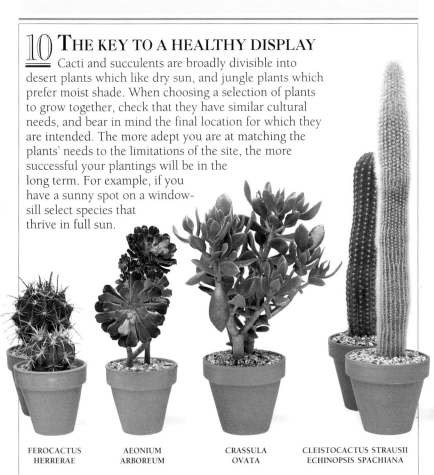

| FEROCACTUS HERRERAE | AEONIUM ARBOREUM | CRASSULA OVATA | CLEISTOCACTUS STRAUSII ECHINOPSIS SPACHIANA |

INDOOR DESERT DISPLAY

11 HOW LONG WILL THE DISPLAY LAST?

Indoor displays are well-suited to the warm, dry conditions of a centrally heated home and will thrive for two to three years. After this, renew the compost and replace outsized plants.

12 HOW TO HANDLE PRICKLY PLANTS

When working with spiny cacti, particularly those with very fine or barbed spines, use thick gloves, a paper collar, or barbecue tongs to prevent your hands from becoming "attached" to the cactus.

PAPER HANDLE METHOD
Fold a length of brown paper into a strip 5 cm (2 in) wide. Wrap the strip around the stem and lift the plant out of its pot.

GLOVED METHOD
Wearing thick gloves, ease the plant out of the pot by supporting the plant in one hand, and turning the pot upside-down.

13 REMOVING SPINES

Use cosmetic tweezers to gently extract spines that become embedded in your skin. To strip out fine bristles which are less visible, pat the affected area with a piece of adhesive tape, or soak in hot soapy water to open the pores.

USING STICKY TAPE TO REMOVE BRISTLES

14 SHAPE CONSIDERATIONS

The decorative appeal of cacti lies in their abstract forms, which range from tiny globes to creeping candle-like stems, to huge column shapes. Other succulents also offer a diversity of forms and include shrub- or tree-like species, or low-lying plants with rosettes of leaves. Some have arching or trailing stems while others have bulbous forms. In bloom, beautiful flower shapes and colours make an attractive addition to any display of cacti and succulents.

△ LITHOPS
KARASMONTANA

◁ ECHEVERIA
ELEGANS

ECHINOPSIS
SPACHIANA ▷

AGAVE
VICTORIA-
REGINAE ▷

CLEISTOCACTUS
STRAUSII ▷

◁ HOYA
CARNOSA × KERRI

ECHINOPSIS
CHAMAECEREUS ▷

△ ECHINOPSIS
HYBRID

△ SENECIO
STAPELIIFORMIS

15 PLANNING THE DESIGN

Choose plants of a similar size
with a variety of shapes, textures,
and colours to add interest. To
arrive at the best result before
planting, try different designs
with the plants still in their pots.

EXPERIMENTING WITH DESIGN

△ FEROCACTUS
HERRERAE

16 CACTI & SUCCULENTS IN CONTAINERS

The slow growth and long display life of cacti and succulents, make them ideal plants to grow in the limited space of a container. Potted plants can also be moved indoors or outdoors, depending on the weather, which suits varieties that are susceptible to cold, damp, and frost. A very wide choice of pots is available. Select a style and material that complements your plants, and group containers for maximum impact.

◁ **EARTHENWARE JARS**
Two columnar cacti in large earthenware jars create a bold but simple display inside or out.

WOVEN BASKETS △
Plant up plastic-lined baskets with small species that offer a variety of texture.

PAINTED POTS ▷
Brightly painted pots filled with strong-shaped cacti make a striking display.

17 CHOOSING A SUITABLE SITE

Take into account practical points as well as aesthetic considerations before deciding on a site. Ensure that the light, temperature, and humidity conditions suit the plants' needs, and check that the plants will be displayed at a height that shows them off to best advantage.

PLANTS DISPLAYED ON A WINDOWSILL

18 PLANTING IN A RAISED BED

Cacti and succulents can be planted outdoors but only in frost-free areas. Choose soil that is free-draining and find a sunny position sheltered from strong winds. To improve drainage, or when planting in a region with high rainfall, build a raised bed or sloping mound.

1 Clear away any topdressing and dig a hole large enough to take the root ball. Gently tease apart the plant's roots.

2 Position the plant to the same depth as it was in its pot. Fill in and firm the soil. Sprinkle with topdressing.

19 PLANTING IN A WALL CREVICE

Gaps in garden walls filled with shallow soil make attractive sites for establishing succulents that are native to rocky habitats. With the aid of a small tool, such as a widger, scrape out some of the soil from the wall crevice. Gently insert the plant's roots, and while holding it in place, fill in with new compost. Firm the plant in position.

20 TOOLS & EQUIPMENT

Thick gloves, a trowel, and pots are the basic equipment required for planting an indoor or outdoor display. Have a dessert spoon to hand when filling in a small display with compost as there is little space between the plants for a trowel. Remove any grit or dust from the plants with a soft paintbrush.

GLOVES △
Choose suede or leather gardening gloves for handling prickly plants.

SPOON △
A large spoon works as a mini-trowel for use in small spaces.

TROWEL ▷
A wide-blade trowel is ideal for mixing potting compost, digging raised beds, and for planting up larger containers.

△ BRUSHES
You will need a fine brush for pollinating and a larger brush for removing dirt without damaging plants.

◁ POTS OF VARYING SIZES
As a rule, cacti and succulents grow slowly and produce shallow roots. Small full-depth pots and shallow pans are ideal.

21 HANGING BASKET DISPLAY

Jungle cacti with arching stems and pendent flowers, and most trailing succulents are well suited to hanging basket displays. To avoid scorching, place in bright indirect light.

1 Sit the basket in a large pot to steady it. Line the basket with moss and a saucer at the base to stop drips. Fill two-thirds of the basket with gritty compost.

CHRISTMAS CACTUS △
Schlumbergera 'Frida' a shade-loving hybrid, produces vivid flowers in winter.

2 Ease each plant out of its pot. Hold the base of the stem in one hand and tease out some of the roots with your fingers, taking care not to damage them.

3 Place three plants in a triangular formation and fill in with compost, firming it down with your fingertips. Do not water for 2–3 days to avoid root rot.

22 WINDOW BOX DISPLAY

The variety of shapes, colours, and textures that distinguish many species of cacti and succulents can be displayed to glorious effect in a window box or trough. Good drainage is key to a long-lasting display that will thrive outside for most of the year. Bring indoors in winter to protect from frosts.

1 △ Cover drainage holes with crocks and a layer of paper to prevent loose compost from clogging up the drainage.

2 △ Half-fill the window box with compost. Take each plant out of its pot and position it so that its root ball is at the same depth as it was in its pot. Fill in with compost, pressing gently.

3 △ Brush off any grit that has fallen onto the leaves. Spoon a layer of gravel over the compost to prevent the surface from drying out and stop algal growth.

THE FINISHED DISPLAY
To recreate this display you need (from left to right): Crassula ovata; Echeveria elegans; Cleistocactus strausii; Aeonium arboreum *'Atropurpureum'*; Ferocactus herrerae; Ferocactus latispinus; Echinopsis spachiana; Mammillaria bombycina.

Place tall plants at the back

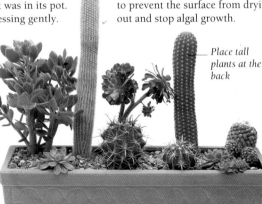

23 PLANTING AN INDOOR BOWL

Small or slow-growing cacti and succulents that favour dry habitats offer enormous scope for creating a low-maintenance desert-style display. Plant in a shallow bowl and position indoors in a brightly lit site and the display will thrive for two or three years before the plants and compost need replacing.

1 △ Mix two parts peat with one part grit to make a free-draining compost. Trowel a thick layer over the bowl base.

2 △ Decide on a design, placing taller species at the back. Plant each species to the same depth as it was in its own pot. Fill in with soil.

3 △ Once all the plants are in place, lightly firm the compost surface. Using a fine brush, remove any compost that is lodged between the plants' leaves.

Add pebbles and a topdressing of grit

INDOOR DISPLAY
For this planting you will need (clockwise from top left): Aeonium haworthii; Opuntia *species;* Echeveria fimbriata; E. elegans; Mammillaria magnimamma. *All those listed above have shallow roots so the bowl need only be 8 cm (3 in) deep. All need very little water and are dormant in winter.*

POT PLANTING

24 WHICH COMPOST?

Cacti and succulents will thrive in a potting compost that is free-draining yet retains moisture. Special proprietary cactus potting composts are ideal, or you can use commercial soil-less compost mixed with grit. Alternatively, make your own soil-less compost from coconut fibre, peat, bark, and grit. Soil-based composts are fine if mixed with grit.

SOIL-LESS COMPOST

SOIL-BASED COMPOST

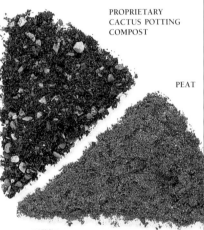

PROPRIETARY CACTUS POTTING COMPOST

PEAT

25 HOW MUCH COMPOST?

All pot-grown plants need to have their roots covered by compost to within 1 cm (½ in) of the rim to enable water and air to reach the roots. In time, compost compacts and the level drops so remember to top it up.

WRONG SOIL LEVEL

CORRECT SOIL LEVEL

26 COMPOST MIXTURES

The extent to which the soil drains and retains water, plus its level of acidity all determine which ingredients need to be added and in what quantities.

INDOOR PLANTS
For indoor plants, mix two parts commercial soil-less compost with one part grit. Soil-based composts are acceptable but tend to become compacted when dry. A good mix is three parts John Innes No.2 compost to one part washed grit.

OUTDOOR PLANTS
Assess the quality of the soil before you plant. The majority of cacti and succulents prefer slightly acid soil. To make soil more acid, add peat or garden compost. If the soil is sandy, add one part peat to three parts soil. Add grit to the improved soil.

OUTDOOR CONTAINERS
For outdoor containers and raised beds, make a soil-less compost out of three parts of either peat, coconut fibre, or wood bark, and one part washed grit; use equal parts of peat and washed grit to fill pots that do not drain easily.

27 IMPROVING DRAINAGE

Good drainage is necessary to prevent root rot in cacti and succulents. When planting up a container, begin by covering each drainage hole with a crock and a layer of clay pellets. Place paper on top to prevent the compost from sticking and impeding drainage.

BROWN PAPER LAYER
Place a sheet of brown paper on top of the clay pellets before adding soil. By the time the soil settles, it will have dissolved.

KITCHEN PAPER TOWEL ALTERNATIVE
A layer of absorbent kitchen towel on top of the clay pellets also prevents the new soil from clogging up the drainage system.

28 WHY APPLY A TOPDRESSING ?

Covering the soil in a topdressing of small gravel or crushed stone has many practical benefits. It helps to conserve moisture in the soil, and prevents the surface from drying out. It suppresses weeds and inhibits the growth of algae. It also reduces soil erosion, and prevents splashmarks on the plants during watering. Topdressings must be inert so do not use limestone which increases the soil's alkalinity.

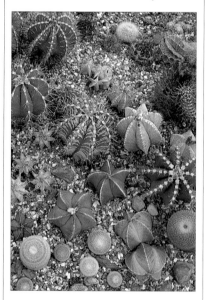

GRAVEL TOPDRESSING
A layer of gravel on top of the soil between plants, retains the moisture in the soil and ensures a low-maintenance, weed-free bed.

29 WHICH TOPDRESSING ?

As well as serving a practical function (*see left*), topdressings are also decorative. It is best, however, to avoid artificially coloured gravels as these detract from the simplicity of the plants.

PEA-SIZED PEBBLES

SMALL GRAVEL

CRUSHED STONE

WATERING

Water only when the meter indicates that the soil is dry

MEASURING THE SOIL MOISTURE

30 KNOWING WHEN TO WATER

Perhaps the most common cause of premature death in cultivated cacti and succulents is overwatering, which rots the roots. Most cacti and succulents can withstand periods of drought so if in any doubt, do not water the plants.

- A moisture meter is the only accurate way to measure how dry or wet the compost is.
- Do not water until the moisture meter indicates almost dry.
- In general, cacti and succulents only need watering when in active growth (usually spring or summer) and need little or no water while dormant (mainly winter months).

31 SURVIVAL WITHOUT WATER

Inappropriate light and temperature are likely to cause permanent physical damage to cacti and succulents but lack of water will not. Cacti deprived of water simply shrink into dormancy as they would in the desert during a drought, and will quickly revive once watered. When the sun is hot, however, shield plants or they will suffer scorch damage which is visible as brown patches.

SCORCH-DAMAGED PLANT

32 WATERING CALENDAR

During the year, the water intake of cacti and succulents varies. During periods of active growth, usually spring or summer, they need water every 1–2 weeks, but in dormant periods they survive with little or no water. The plants' seasonal needs are indicated below.

Can with rose is used for outside plants

Increase humidity with a spray-mister

Use small can to water indoor plants

SPRING
In spring, water most plants every 1–2 weeks; indoor plants in small pots need more frequent watering as the soil tends to dry out more quickly. Outdoor plantings, window boxes, and pots, especially those with a topdressing, retain water longer and often need less.

SUMMER
In summer, allow soil or compost to dry out almost completely between waterings. It is very important not to overwater in hot weather as most cacti and succulents become dormant. In this state, they are unable to take up water, and if left in wet compost, rot from the roots up.

AUTUMN
As in the spring months, autumn is a period of active growth, and most plants need watering every 1–2 weeks.

WINTER
In areas where the temperature is above 10°C (50°F) water plants sparingly; in cooler regions stop watering altogether.

33 WHAT TIME OF DAY TO WATER

The best time of day to water is early in the morning or late afternoon so that the plants have time to absorb the water and any surplus moisture on the leaves or stems before the sun comes out. Watering in full sun can scorch the leaves and eventually kills the plant.

WATER PLANTS OUT OF SUNLIGHT

34 INCREASING HUMIDITY

Most cacti and succulents favour a dry atmosphere but jungle species thrive in hot, damp environments. To recreate this indoors, or in a conservatory or greenhouse, the temperature must be in the range of 21–32°C (70–90°F). Create a high level of moisture in the atmosphere, by gently misting the plant's leaves with a hand-held spray. Continue to use a spray-mister as part of your watering routine. Like other succulents, these plants can survive drought.

SPRAY-MISTING AN EPIPHYTIC CACTUS

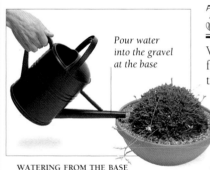

Pour water into the gravel at the base

WATERING FROM THE BASE

35 WATERING METHODS

Water a large collection of plants from overhead with a light spray to prevent soil from becoming dislodged. If you have only a few plants in pots, gently pour water into the gravel top-soil to avoid splash back. Take care not to overwater as this may eventually result in root rot.

36 SIGNS OF STEM ROT

Cacti and succulents that are kept in unsuitably cold or damp conditions, or that have poor roots, are prone to rot. Rot fungus penetrates the plant's skin and attacks the tissue, turning it soft and eventually black. If stem rot attacks your pot plants, cut off any healthy stems for cuttings, and destroy the rest. If rot attacks the stems of permanent outdoor plantings, apply copper sulphate.

FEEDING

37 WHY FEED DESERT PLANTS?

In the wild, the sporadic and unbalanced availability of minerals means that desert plants just survive but in cultivation, with regular feeding, they soon flourish. During the growing season, cacti and succulents benefit from regular supplies of nitrogen for good top-growth, potassium for flowers, and phosphorus for strong root growth.

FLOWERING DESERT PLANTS
Although able to survive in the desert on a low-mineral diet, cultivated cacti will thrive if fed during the growing season.

38 WHEN TO FEED

Cacti and succulents require feeding in two stages. At planting time, mix a base fertilizer into the compost or soil. Then apply either liquid or solid fertilizers with routine waterings, but no more than weekly for desert plants or twice weekly for jungle species.

39 WHICH FERTILIZER?

Fertilizers are available from nurseries in powder, granular, liquid, or solid form. They may be organic or inorganic. Organic fertilizers include seaweed, and though rich in trace elements, their chemical content is less consistent than their inorganic counterparts.

◁ HOUSE PLANT TABLETS

FEED STICKS ▽

△ FEED TABLETS

▽ LIQUID FERTILIZER

△ SPECIALIST FERTILIZER GRANULES

SPECIALIST ▷ FERTILIZER POWDER

40 SHORT-TERM FEEDING

Cacti and succulents respond well in the short term to tomato liquid fertilizer, if diluted to half strength. Do not use as a long-term solution because its low nitrogen content, (only one to five per cent of the fertilizer) can cause cacti and succulents to become stunted.

41 SIGNS OF OVERFEEDING

You can tell by the changes in the physical appearance of cacti and succulents when they are being overfed with minerals, such as nitrogen. Cacti become thin and reluctant to produce flowers, while succulents produce spindly, lank, unattractive growth.

LIGHT

42 HOW MUCH LIGHT?

Most cacti and succulents need full sun during active periods of growth in order to stay healthy. They tolerate lower light levels in winter when they are dormant but even then need a bright position. When cultivating cacti and other succulents indoors, place plants directly in front of a window or in a conservatory. Natural daylight can be supplemented by artificial lights.

WHERE TO POSITION PLANTS IN A ROOM
Most desert cacti and succulents require bright natural light throughout the year. The area directly in front of a window is best, any further away is too dark.

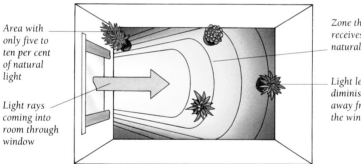

Area with only five to ten per cent of natural light

Light rays coming into room through window

Zone that receives most natural light

Light levels diminish away from the window

PALE SKIN DUE TO INADEQUATE LIGHT

43 THE EFFECTS OF POOR LIGHT

Poor light and incorrect feeding of cacti and succulents produces one of two ill effects, either the skin turns pale and growth is elongated, or stunted leaves on spindly shoots result. To resume healthy growth, prune back affected stems and place the plant in bright light.

44 LIGHT-SENSITIVE PLANTS

A few cacti and some succulents are so light sensitive that they do not flower unless there are less than 12 hours of daylight. Even artificial light prevents flowering, so keep the plants in a little-used room until they bud.

Flowers open in winter

Flower colour is affected by light

◁ CRASSULA FALCATA

Flowers open in late summer

△ SCHLUMBERGERA 'FIRECRACKER'

Fleshy silver-grey leaves

Glossy leaves dark green on top and deep red underneath

△ CRASSULA STREYI

45 PROVIDING LIGHT IN WINTER

Cacti and succulents tolerate less light in the winter months, when many are dormant, but even shade-loving *Epiphyllum* favour a bright position. Place a mirror behind the plant to help provide an even light, or buy special artificial lights from a good garden centre with wavelengths that have been adjusted to suit the plant's needs.

46 PLANTS TO GROW IN FULL SUN

Choose desert plants that thrive in dry conditions in full sun. These species are best cultivated outdoors in warmer climates with a minimum temperature of 16°C (61°F). Otherwise, they grow well in a sunny indoor site, such as on a windowsill or in a greenhouse.

◁ MAMMILLARIA PARKINSONII

A sun-loving cactus that bears a ring of flowers and red seed pods in spring or early summer

This species from Mexico produces bright yellow flowers

◁ ASTROPHYTUM MYRIOSTIGMA

PLANTS FOR FULL SUN
CACTI
Ariocarpus species
Astrophytum species
Cephalocereus species
Cleistocactus species
Echinopsis species
Mammillaria parkinsonii
SUCCULENTS
Agave utahensis
Aloe dichotoma
Conophytum species
Cyphostemma species
Gibbaeum species
Lampranthus species

47 AVOID LEAF SCORCH

In summer, even plants that enjoy full sun can be susceptible to leaf scorch, especially if they are cultivated in a greenhouse. Fit blinds to the glass roof so that you can provide some protection, and when moving young plants out into full sun, cover in fabric until they have acclimatized.

△ ALOE DICHOTOMA

Spiky leaves can be blue, grey, or deep green

Flowers open on summer nights

△ AGAVE UTAHENSIS

Plant grows best in warmer climates

ECHINOPSIS ▷
MAMILLOSA
F. KERMESINA

48 PLANTS FOR DRY SHADE

These are predominantly desert plants that need dry conditions in diffuse rather than direct sun to flourish. Some of these plants are prone to rot if they become wet, and their leaves may scorch if exposed to the sun's rays for long periods.

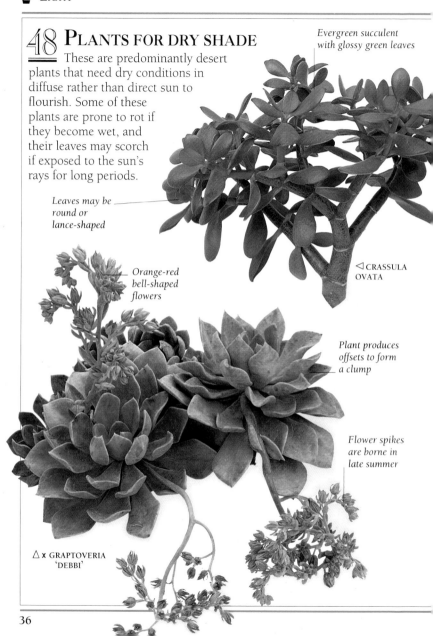

Evergreen succulent with glossy green leaves

Leaves may be round or lance-shaped

◁ CRASSULA OVATA

Orange-red bell-shaped flowers

Plant produces offsets to form a clump

Flower spikes are borne in late summer

△ x GRAPTOVERIA 'DEBBI'

PLANTS FOR DRY SHADE
CACTI
Echinopsis chamaecereus
f. *lutea*
SUCCULENTS
Ceropegia woodii
Crassula ovata
Echeveria setosa
Euphorbia species
Gasteria species
Graptopetalum bellum
x *Graptoveria* 'Debbi'
Haworthia attenuata
Huernia species
Kalanchoe blossfeldiana

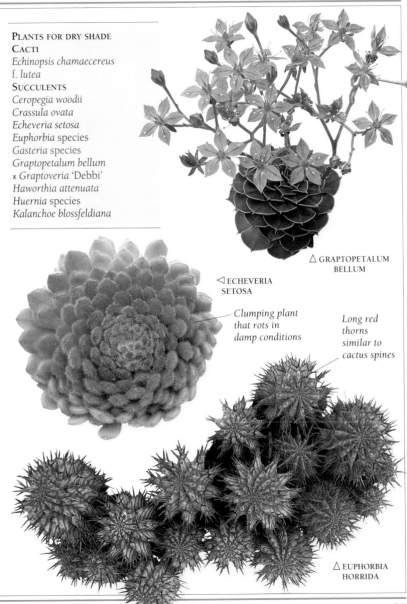

△ GRAPTOPETALUM
BELLUM

◁ ECHEVERIA
SETOSA

*Clumping plant
that rots in
damp conditions*

*Long red
thorns
similar to
cactus spines*

△ EUPHORBIA
HORRIDA

49 PLANTS FOR MOIST SHADE

Not all cacti favour direct sunlight and dry conditions. Some cacti, known as epiphytic, obtain moisture and nutrients from the atmosphere, so flourish in greenhouses where light filters through, and there is a high moisture content. Their natural habitat is below the tree canopy of a rainforest or jungle and, because of this, they have long leaves to absorb maximum light. Spray-mist often to increase humidity.

◁ APOROCACTUS FLAGELLIFORMIS

▽ x APOROPHYLLUM 'DAWN'

Stems grow up to 30 cm (12 in) in a year

Larger flowers than Aporocactus species

PLANTS FOR MOIST SHADE
CACTI
Aporocactus flagelliformis
x *Aporophyllum*, most hybrids including
x *A.* 'Dawn'
x *A.* 'Sussex Flame'
Epiphyllum hybrids
Heliocereus species
Rhipsalis species
Schlumbergera species
Selenicereus species
SUCCULENTS
Aeonium species

TEMPERATURE

50 TEMPERATURE FOR ACTIVE GROWTH

Most cacti species and some succulents grow in summer and are dormant in winter, but extremes of temperature – either hot or cold – can shock the plants into dormancy at any time of year. Most cacti and succulents need a temperature of 16°C (61°F) to grow, while tropical plants need higher temperatures of 21–32°C (70–90°F).

PLANTS GROWING BEHIND GLASS
When mature, most cacti and succulents need full sun and warmth for growth. A sunny windowsill is the perfect site.

51 REVIVING COLD-DAMAGED PLANTS

A few cacti and succulents tolerate outdoor temperatures as low as 0°C (32°F) for very short periods but long periods of low temperatures can damage the soft, new growth of most plants, scar their tissue, and they will eventually collapse. To revive cold-damaged plants, increase the temperature to dry out dead tissue and prevent rot attack. If possible, cut out affected areas.

SCARRING ON STEM DUE TO COLD DAMAGE

52 DRAUGHT-FREE VENTILATION

In a greenhouse environment, provide draught-free ventilation in summer and winter for healthy plant growth. Ventilation reduces a build up of moisture in the air, which can cause rot in many cacti. Plants grown in the house will also appreciate being moved outdoors into the fresh air in summer.

53 PROTECTION FROM FROST

Most cacti and succulents only grow well outdoors if the temperature does not fall below 5°C (41°F). To protect plants from occasional frosts in normally frost-free areas, wrap them in paper, plastic, or sacking. If cold damage occurs, it tends to attack only soft new growth which can be cut out.

Columnar plants are especially vulnerable

Wrap up the entire length of the stem in brown paper

Fasten at intervals with raffia

PROTECTING TALL CACTI FROM FROST

54 PLANTS FOR WARM CLIMATES

These are cacti and succulents that are sensitive to cold climates and will only flourish if the temperature throughout the year does not fall below 16°C (61°F). In temperate regions, cultivate these plants indoors only, or in summer grow them outside in containers. Bring them inside, before the cold weather arrives, to avoid the danger of frost damage.

Rust red spines grow densely on unusual double crown

△ MELOCACTUS MATANZANUS

Spines fade with age

Dark glossy leaves with pale downy underside

Flowers are produced from spring to autumn

Leaves have prominent veins

ADENIUM ▷ OBESUM

Stem has toxic milky sap

PLANTS FOR WARM CLIMATES
CACTI
Echinocactus grusonii
Echinopsis chamaecereus f. *lutea*
Epiphyllum crenatum
Gymnocalycium mihanovichii 'Red Top'
Melocactus matanzanus
Rhipsalis crispata
SUCCULENTS
Adenium obesum
Brachystelma barberae
Caralluma species
Ceropegia woodii
Cyphostemma bainesii
Monadenium species
Pachypodium namaquanum
Sanseviera trifasciata

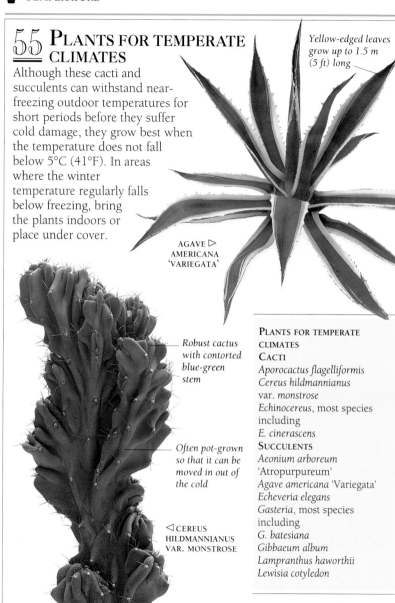

55 PLANTS FOR TEMPERATE CLIMATES

Although these cacti and succulents can withstand near-freezing outdoor temperatures for short periods before they suffer cold damage, they grow best when the temperature does not fall below 5°C (41°F). In areas where the winter temperature regularly falls below freezing, bring the plants indoors or place under cover.

Yellow-edged leaves grow up to 1.5 m (5 ft) long

AGAVE ▷
AMERICANA
'VARIEGATA'

Robust cactus with contorted blue-green stem

Often pot-grown so that it can be moved in out of the cold

◁ CEREUS
HILDMANNIANUS
VAR. MONSTROSE

PLANTS FOR TEMPERATE CLIMATES
CACTI
Aporocactus flagelliformis
Cereus hildmannianus var. *monstrose*
Echinocereus, most species including
E. cinerascens
SUCCULENTS
Aeonium arboreum 'Atropurpureum'
Agave americana 'Variegata'
Echeveria elegans
Gasteria, most species including
G. batesiana
Gibbaeum album
Lampranthus haworthii
Lewisia cotyledon

Hybrid valued for its quill-like leaves

56 PLANTS FOR COLD CLIMATES

There are a few species of succulents that are hardy enough to survive winter temperatures as low as -15°C (5°F), but only if they are kept dry or are protected by a layer of insulating snow. Most of these hardy plants are small bushes or carpeting plants and make good year-round ground cover.

Swollen leaves protected by a downy layer

A hardy alpine well-suited to rock gardens

SEMPERVIVUM △ 'ODDITY'

Symmetrical rosette of pointed, scale-like leaves that turn from green to purple

PLANTS FOR COLD CLIMATES
SUCCULENTS
Sedum, many hardy
species including
S. acre
S. album
S. cauticolum
S. spectabile
S. spurium
Sempervivum,
most hybrids and species
including
S. arachnoideum
S. 'Emerson's Giant'
S. 'Oddity'

SEMPERVIVUM
'EMERSON'S GIANT' ▷

43

MAINTENANCE

57 CLEANING NON-HAIRY PLANTS

An indoor display will last for two or three years before it needs replanting, and in that time dust will collect on the leaf surface. To keep the smooth, shiny leaves common to many succulents looking healthy, gently dust them from time to time with a soft artist's brush. For best results, dust carefully between any small gaps.

DUSTING LEAVES WITH A PAINT BRUSH

58 DUSTING SPINY PLANTS

Many cacti are grown indoors on sunny window-ledges and, like any beautiful object, they soon start to gather dust. As well as looking unsightly, a thick layer of dust may prevent the plant from converting sunlight into chlorophyll during photosynthesis and, in time, this may impede growth. An effective way to remove dust from spiny plants is with a hairdryer. This way your hands do not have to come into contact with the spines. Set the hairdryer to a slow, cool setting and holding the dryer about 15 cm (6 in) from the plant, gently blow away the dust.

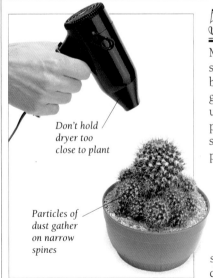

Don't hold dryer too close to plant

Particles of dust gather on narrow spines

BLOWING AWAY DUST PARTICLES

59 DEADHEADING

After flowering, deadheading is necessary to maintain both the appearance and health of the plant. The easiest way to deadhead is with your fingers. Grip the flower between your thumb and forefinger and carefully pinch it off. This process may have to be repeated several times during the flowering season.

PINCHING OFF DEAD FLOWERHEADS

PLUCKING OFF A DAMAGED LEAF

60 REMOVING DEAD LEAVES OR SHOOTS

Dead or damaged leaves or shoots may harbour pests and diseases. Good hygiene involves removing these dead or damaged areas to keep the plant in good condition. With rosette-shaped succulents, grip the leaf at its base close to the stem and pull it off cleanly. Pinch out shoots above a healthy joint.

61 CUTTING OUT DAMAGED AREAS

Cacti and succulents can become damaged if their cultural needs are not met. The leaves and stems of succulents growing close to the roots turn brown and may have to be removed if the rest of the plant is to survive. Using secateurs, cut out the problem stems. When all the damaged matter has been dealt with, feed and water correctly.

TRIMMING WITH SECATEURS

62 WHY PRUNE?

Most succulents and some leafy cacti need pruning to keep their shape and to produce new shoots. Pruning removes straggly growth that impairs the plant's vigour, and makes it less open to attack by pests. Prune shrubby succulents in spring, winter-flowering succulents in summer, and leafy epiphytic cacti after flowering. If pruned often, plants become woody and need replacing.

63 HOW TO PRUNE

Always use a sharp pair of secateurs when pruning. Blunt pruning tools create ragged cuts that may become infected. Trim shrubby plants to just above a shoot or bud. To improve the look of mounding or creeping plants, remove old brown foliage from beneath new growth. For trailing plants, cut back long stems to encourage bushy growth near the stem base. Frequently pruned succulents may become woody.

STRAGGLY GROWTH NEEDS PRUNING

1 Select top-heavy leaves that have branched out from the parent stem. Using sharp anvil secateurs, cut straight across the stem just below the leaf joint. To prevent disease, cut as close as you can to the joint and do not leave a stub.

2 Using clean, straight cuts, prune out old, stunted, or diseased stems that are situated at the base of the plant and are unlikely to produce a crop of flowers.

3 To prevent the death of shoot tips (dieback), remove any brown stem ends. Cut across the healthy section of the stem just below the brown tip.

4 To encourage new flowering shoots, prune back old stems that have already flowered until they are level with young shoots. Make an angled cut across the vein of the old leaf, at a point just above where the new shoot begins.

PRUNED INTO SHAPE

64 WHY REPOT?

All cacti and succulents need repotting from time to time for the following reasons: to allow enough room for maximum root growth – cramped roots cannot take up nutrients and growth is soon inhibited; to loosen compacted soil so that air and water can circulate; and to correct the mineral imbalance caused by long-term watering and feeding.

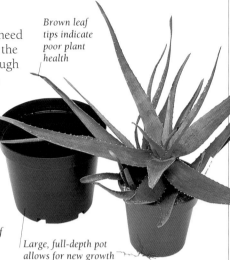

Brown leaf tips indicate poor plant health

Large, full-depth pot allows for new growth

PLANT IN NEED OF REPOTTING ▷
Roots growing out through the base of the pot are a sure sign that this fast-growing succulent needs repotting.

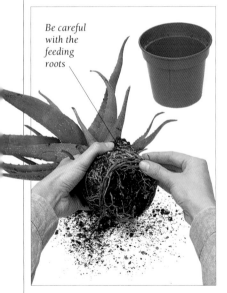

Be careful with the feeding roots

65 TEASING OUT POT-BOUND ROOTS

Take the plant out of its container and examine its roots for disease. Handle with care as plants that have not been repotted for years, or those kept in too wet or too dry conditions often have poor, fragile root systems. If the root ball has become compacted and you intend to plant it in the same type of compost as in the original pot, break up the root ball to help the roots grow. If using a different compost, first shake off the old.

◁ **LOOSENING A COMPACTED ROOT BALL**
Prepare the plant for repotting by teasing out compacted roots. Examine the roots and cut out any that are old or damaged.

66 HOW TO REPOT A CACTUS

The best time to repot cacti and succulents is at the start of the growing season. Choose a clean pot that is large enough to accommodate new growth. Plants smaller than 15 cm (6 in) are best grown in half pots 2.5 cm (1 in) wider than the plant's diameter; taller plants need full-depth pots 5–10 cm (2–4 in) wider than the plant's diameter.

1 Scrub the pot with soapy water so that it is germ-free. Place a little compost in the base and use another pot to mark the size of the plant's roots.

2 Fill in between the two pots with compost to within 1 cm (½ in) of the rims. Press down on the inner pot to firm the compost and to leave a hole.

3 Lie the plant on its side and twist off the old pot. Remove any old loose compost from the root ball and tease out the roots. Cut out any dead roots.

4 Holding the plant at the top of the root ball, carefully drop it into the hole. Straighten it and lightly firm the compost. Sprinkle with topdressing.

PROPAGATION

67 WHY PROPAGATE?

Propagation is a low-cost way of obtaining new cacti and succulent plants and it is the only way to increase the presence of rare and endangered species. There are several methods: taking cuttings or dividing a plant to reproduce hybrids; raising from seed which yields new plant types; and grafting which suits more difficult species.

CLEARLY LABEL YOUNG PLANTS

68 RAISING FROM SEED

For best results, grow plants from fresh seed rather than old commercial seed. Collect the seed from the plants after the seed pods have ripened. Squash the wet seed on to a paper towel and leave to dry. When dry, sieve the seed to remove chaff that may cause rot.

1 Fill a pot to the brim with cactus potting compost and firm. Scatter the seed over the soil. Stand the pot in tepid water. Allow to drain, and then topdress.

2 Label the pot and cover in a plastic bag. Leave in bright shade with a minimum temperature of 19°C (66°F), or 21–27°C (70–81°F) for faster results.

69 SOWING LARGE SEEDS

Small seeds can be sprinkled over the soil surface but larger seeds need to be pressed down into the compost until they sit at twice their own depth. Allow at least 1 cm (½ in) between each seed so that they have room to develop. Some of the larger seeds have a thick outer coating. Before sowing, put these seeds in a refrigerator for 48 hours.

PLANTING LARGE SEEDS

70 PRICKING OUT SEEDLINGS

When the seeds germinate in about 2–4 weeks, remove the plastic bag to improve ventilation. Grow them on at a minimum temperature of 10°C (50°F) in a bright situation but out of direct sunlight which may scorch young plants. When the seedlings are big enough to be handled without damaging their roots (several months to a year, depending on the species), prick them out. Plant seedlings less than 2.5 cm (1 in) in trays and larger ones in pots.

1 Prick out seedlings when they begin to crowd each other. Using a widger, gently ease small clumps with their compost out of the pot.

2 Taking care not to damage the delicate roots, separate each seedling from the clump, saving as much compost as possible with the roots.

3 Almost fill several 5 cm (2 in) pots with cactus potting mix. Plant each seedling in a pot and dress with grit. Water 3–4 days later.

71 CROSS-POLLINATION

For plants to produce seed, pollen must be carried from the flowers of one plant to another. Outdoors, this is achieved naturally but under-cover plants need cross-pollinating by hand. First isolate the flower to protect it from other plants' pollen.

1 ▷ When ripe and laden with pollen, gently dab the anthers with a fine artist's brush to pick up pollen.

Stigma
Stamen
Anther

2 △ Carefully brush the pollen on to the stigma of a flower on another plant of the same species. When seeds form, collect and label them with their parentage details.

72 TAKING LEAF CUTTINGS

A quick and simple method of propagating succulents, such as *Gasteria* and some *Haworthia,* is to take leaf cuttings. Take the cuttings when the plant starts active growth and it will take root in 3–12 weeks.

1 Holding the plant steady, select a young healthy leaf and pull it away from the stem. Place the leaf to dry in a warm, dry site for a day or two, or until a callus has formed over the wound.

2 Fill a small pot with cactus potting compost to within 5 cm (2 in) of the rim. Set the leaf in the soil and cover the surface in grit. Keep the pot just damp, in partial shade at 18°C (64°F).

73 TAKING STEM CUTTINGS

Many succulents, except those that have water-storing tissue in a swollen rootstock, are propagated in this way. Take stem cuttings in spring when a plant starts active growth, and avoid long cuttings which wilt before they take root.

2 △ Trim the cut stem so that it is only 5–10 cm (2–4 in) long. Remove any leaves from the base. Place the stem in a warm site until a callus forms on the cut.

1 △ Choose a healthy sturdy stem. Steady the plant and then using a small, sharp knife, slice the stem just above a bud or a new shoot. Do not leave a stub.

3 △ Plant the cutting in a small pot one third-full of cactus potting compost and the remainder grit. Keep just moist in an airy, bright site for 2–6 weeks.

74 HOW TO STOP BLEEDING STEMS

When cut or wounded, all *Euphorbia* and some succulents in the family *Asclepiadaceae* produce a milky white sap. To stop the flow of stems that bleed, dip the cut end in tepid water for a few seconds. Avoid getting sap on your skin as it can cause irritation. If the parent plant is bleeding, hold a damp cloth against the wound.

75 TAKING STEM SECTIONS

Plants that have flattened, leaf-like stems, such as *Epiphyllum*, and many columnar cacti, can be propagated from a section of stem rather than a complete stem. The section should be taken at the end of the dormant period and usually takes 3–12 weeks to root.

1 Using a clean, sharp knife, cut a stem into 23 cm (9 in) sections. Place in a warm, dry place to form calluses.

2 Fill a small pot, one third full of cactus potting compost and the rest grit. Insert the bottom end of the stem.

76 DIVISION OF CLUMP-FORMING OFFSETS

Some cacti, for example, *Mammillaria* and *Echinopsis*, and succulents, such as *Haworthia* and *Gasteria*, grow to form a clump of leaves with many offsets. Those offsets which develop roots can be divided off from the parent plant in spring, and grown on as new plants.

1 Using a widger, carefully dig out and pull away larger offsets from the parent plant. Dust the stem wound with fungicide and leave the offset to callus.

2 Fill a small pot with compost and insert the offset to the same depth as it sat in the parent pot. Topdress with grit and place in sun or bright shade.

77 DIVISION OF OFFSET TUBERS

Succulents with tuberous roots, such as *Senecio* and *Ceropegia* form other tubers, offset from the parent plant, just below soil level.

To obtain new plants, divide up these offsets and grow them on. Water sparingly until the roots are established to avoid rot.

1 Dig down into the compost with a widger to locate an offset tuber. Sever it from the main tuber and lift out.

2 Leave the tuber to callus. If it has roots, plant it in cactus potting mix. If not, use grit with only a little compost.

78 DIVISION OF ROOTSTOCKS

This method of division is used for species that have swollen rootstocks with several growing points. Division is undertaken when the plant is dormant. This propagation method is also used to retain variegated colour on plants grown from cultivars of *Sanseviera*.

1 Dig up the parent plant (*Sanseviera trifasciata*), or remove it from its pot. Cut the rootstock into sections, making sure each one has its own growing point.

2 Cut away any part of the rootstock that is damaged. Dust the cuts with fungicide and leave to callus. Replant each section in cactus potting compost.

79 SPLIT-GRAFTING

A technique for propagating difficult and slow-growing cacti, whereby the top growth of the plant is grafted on to the rootstock of a more vigorous species. When grafted, the growth rate can be increased ten fold. Leafy cacti, such as *Schlumbergera*, respond well to split-grafting if propagated at the start of the spring growing season.

1 Cleanly slice off the top 2.5 cm (1 in) of a vigorous rootstock to form a base on which a plant can be grafted.

2 Make a vertical incision 1–2 cm (½–¾ in) deep, passing through the central core tissue of the rootstock.

3 Select a healthy stem for grafting (1–2 leaf sections long if it is a *Schlumbergera*). Cut it across the joint of the leaf.

4 Trim away the lower 1 cm (½ in). Slice away the skin from both sides until it tapers to fit into the split in the stock.

5 Wedge the prepared cutting (scion) into the split in the rootstock. Ensure that both central core tissues make contact.

6 Push a spine through both pieces to hold the scion in place, and bind with raffia. Leave to grow in a bright, airy site.

80 FLAT-GRAFTING

This method of grafting is used to propagate most types of cacti with contorted growth habits, and those whose seedlings may lack chlorophyll. Choose a healthy cactus for a rootstock; *Echinopsis* species work well. When preparing the graft, ensure that your hands are clean, as cut surfaces are easily infected by fungal diseases.

1 Using a clean knife, slice to a depth of 2.5 cm (1 in) below the crown of the stock, to expose the core tissue.

2 Remove about 6 mm (¼ in) of skin from around the edges of the stock to ensure both core tissues will make contact.

3 Cut off the scion and bevel away 6 mm (¼ in) of skin from around the edges to reveal the core tissue.

START OF NEW GROWTH

4 Place the cut surfaces of the scion and stock together and rotate the scion to remove any air pockets. Fasten together with rubber bands and within two weeks the graft will start to grow.

PESTS & DISEASES

81 IDENTIFYING FUNGAL DISEASES

Although cacti and other succulents are not prone to disease, damp and poor ventilation under cover produces the conditions in which fungal spores thrive, as does the failure to remove damaged leaves or stems. Most fungal infections occur during late spring or autumn. On these cold nights, condensation collects on the leaves of plants cultivated indoors and out and fails to evaporate by morning. Fungal spores develop in beads of water and attack the plant tissue.

FUNGAL LEAF SPOT
Brown spots appear and, if not dealt with, result in leaf drop. Burn infected leaves and treat the plant with copper sulphate.

CORKY SCAB
Cork-like spots develop near the stem base due to disease damage in the past or poor cultivation. Improve growing conditions.

82 PREVENTATIVE MEASURES

If cultivated in the right environment and properly cared for, cacti and succulents should stay healthy. Inspect plants from time to time so that any signs of ill-health can be quickly remedied. Carefully check new plants for pests and diseases to avoid their spread.

83 COMMON PESTS

Pests are a common problem that can be controlled by chemical insecticides or, when plants are cultivated in a greenhouse, by introducing a natural predator. Systemic insecticides are successful because they are absorbed into the plant sap, poisoning any insect that feeds on the plant. During the growing season, use a systemic insecticide 2–3 times as a simple preventative measure. Water the solution on to the plant's roots, not its stem, as its waxy skin will just repel any moisture. If an infestation appears, use weekly for 3–4 weeks.

RED SPIDER MITE DAMAGE
This mite thrives in dry, hot greenhouses, attacking young growth. Increase the humidity or use a predator mite to kill it.

SCALE INSECTS
Attacks stems and lower leaves. Plant growth is checked and sooty mould quickly appears. Treat with a systemic insecticide.

MEALY BUGS
White nests and a sticky honeydew cover infested plants. Treat with a systemic insecticide or, in temperatures above 21°C (70°F), introduce a predator ladybird.

SLUGS & SNAILS
Holes in leaves and slimy trails are signs of slug or snail infestation. Epiphytes that favour damp, shady places are vulnerable, so scatter slug pellets between the plants.

FAVOURITE CACTI

84 x **APOROPHYLLUM**

Ideal plants for hanging baskets, this collection of hybrids is distinguished by its large, open-faced flowers in brilliant shades of orange, cerise, scarlet, purple, and also white. The slender stems grow over 2 m (6 ft) long. Simple to grow, the plants need a fairly rich compost, shade, and temperatures no lower than 6°C (43°F). They flower best if fed during spring and summer.

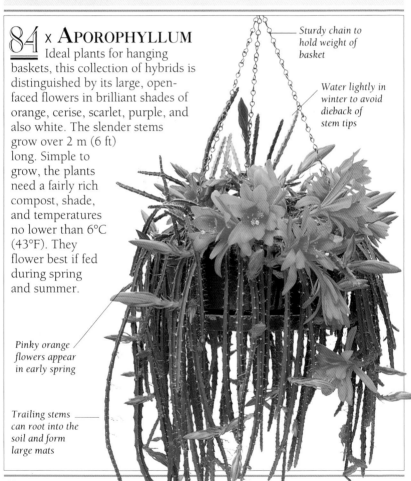

Sturdy chain to hold weight of basket

Water lightly in winter to avoid dieback of stem tips

Pinky orange flowers appear in early spring

Trailing stems can root into the soil and form large mats

85 ECHINOCEREUS KNIPPELIANUS

A striking cactus that produces pink flowers and green berries near the stem tips in spring. The swollen, dark green stems are slow-growing, reaching a spread of 38 cm (15 in). It grows best in temperatures no lower than 5°C (41°F), and prefers bright shade to sun; in the wild, the roots pull the plant below ground to avoid hot sun.

Clump of mature slow-growing stems

Needle-like spines grow from white areoles

86 ECHINOPSIS 'FORTY-NINER'

Like other *Echinopsis* hybrids, this sun-loving, globular cactus was bred to produce a large plant with vivid yellow flowers. The blooms are night-flowering and open at dusk. The flowers fade within 24 hours, but produce several flushes of flowers throughout spring and summer. This cactus is incredibly robust and can withstand neglect and near-freezing winter temperatures as low as 2°C (36°F).

Spiny necks can be 25 cm (10 in) long

Vivid yellow flowers open at dusk

87 GYMNOCALYCIUM HORSTII

Flowers only open fully in bright light

A small, globular cactus, that flowers freely when young from late spring to the end of summer. Waxy, plum-shaped, green fruits appear soon after. Position this cactus in bright shade rather than full sun, which may scorch the plant's skin and stunt its growth, and protect it from winter cold and frost.

88 MAMMILLARIA HAHNIANA

This sun-loving cactus flowers prolifically, even when young, making it a good species to have in a collection. It is commonly known as "birthday cake cactus", because after it has flowered in spring, red seed pods appear and stand in a ring on the crown of the cactus like candles on a cake.

89 MATUCANA INTERTEXTA

A small, globe-shaped cactus with brown needle-like spines. It produces bright red or orange flowers with long necks. The cactus does not flower until the plant is 3–5 years old and then the blooms appear in spring, or summer or sometimes in both seasons. *Matucana* species grow well in sunny sites, with a minimum temperature of 10°C (50°F) to avoid cold damage and root rot. When mature, the plant may develop into a clump.

90 NEOPORTERIA CLAVATA

A further sun-loving, globular cactus that flowers freely – once the plant has reached a diameter of 5–8 cm (2–3 in) – in spring and then again in autumn. Keep this cactus at a temperature above 10°C (50°F). Lightly water it at intervals during the dormant winter period to prevent the roots from drying out and to guard against scarring.

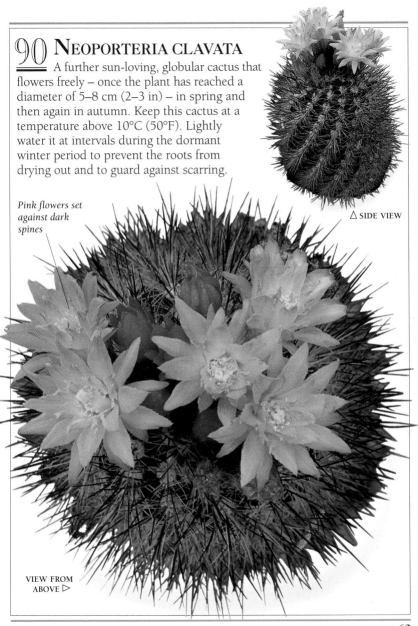

△ SIDE VIEW

Pink flowers set against dark spines

VIEW FROM
ABOVE ▷

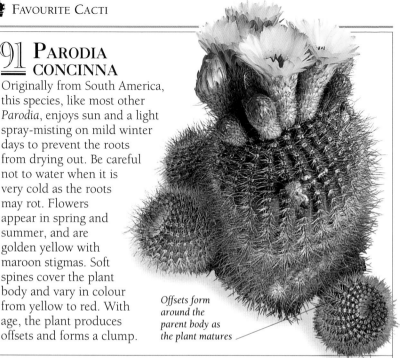

91 PARODIA CONCINNA

Originally from South America, this species, like most other *Parodia*, enjoys sun and a light spray-misting on mild winter days to prevent the roots from drying out. Be careful not to water when it is very cold as the roots may rot. Flowers appear in spring and summer, and are golden yellow with maroon stigmas. Soft spines cover the plant body and vary in colour from yellow to red. With age, the plant produces offsets and forms a clump.

Offsets form around the parent body as the plant matures

92 STENOCACTUS MULTICOSTATUS

The beauty of this cactus lies in the delicate pink flowers with darker pink stripes that grow from the plant crown in spring and summer. These blooms are set against a mass of copper-brown spines. *Stenocactus* species are sun-loving and cannot withstand temperatures lower than 5°C (41°F). Position them where they can be viewed from above to enjoy their spectacular floral display.

FAVOURITE SUCCULENTS

93 AEONIUM ARBOREUM 'SCHWARTZKOPF'

This fast-growing, rosette-shaped succulent with dark purple leaves, makes a good feature plant for summer borders. It is fairly robust and can withstand cold conditions, although damp causes rot. If planted in a bright position, it retains its colour throughout the winter.

Growing point at centre of mature rosette

94 AGAVE VICTORIA-REGINAE

This robust succulent is fairly commonplace as it enjoyed an early popularity in cultivation. Although slow-growing, it produces an attractive domed rosette of dark green leaves, each tipped with a spine and edged and patterned in white. Small flowers appear after 20–30 years when the plant reaches a diameter of 60–90 cm (2–3 ft). Although sun-loving, it can tolerate temperatures as low as 2°C (36°F).

95 ALOE PLICATILIS

Narrow blue-green leaves form a fan shape

A sun-loving succulent that grows to form a large bush or tree with a spread of 3 m (10 ft). Although dormant over summer, this species flowers annually from late spring through to summer with sparse red or orange-red blooms.

Grows to become a large bush or tree

96 CRASSULA ARBORESCENS

A commonly cultivated fleshy-leaved succulent that matures into a bush 3 m (10 ft) high with a spread of 1.2 m (4 ft). The blue-green leaves of this large species are thick and waxy and, if grown in sun, the leaf edges have red margins. Prune this *Crassula* regularly to prevent the leaves weighing down the stem. Long-lasting pink flowers appear in late autumn and provide good winter colour.

97 DUDLEYA BRITTONII

A flower-like succulent with a relatively slow-growing small rosette of silver white leaves. In winter, its silvery bloom is even more pronounced, and at this time of year it is best kept dry. The minimum temperature it can tolerate is 10 °C (50°F). In summer, masses of small, pale yellow flowers are borne on 90 cm (3 ft) stems.

98 ECHEVERIA TUNDELLII

This attractive and easy to grow species, produces offsets of soft blue rosettes that develop into a small mound. The rosettes begin to flower when they are only 2.5 cm (1 in) in diameter, and produce brilliant flame-red flowers.

Generally sun-loving, *Echeveria* are more intensely coloured when grown outdoors, but they make good houseplants for a bright site.

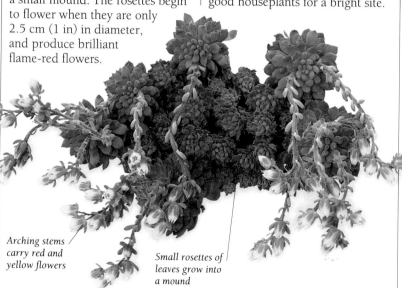

Arching stems carry red and yellow flowers

Small rosettes of leaves grow into a mound

99 HAWORTHIA COARCTATA VAR. ADELAIDENSIS

Haworthia are predominantly rosette-shaped species but this is one of the few plants in the genus to form clumps of tough leafy columns. Its interest lies in its ability to change colour: in cooler weather when it starts to grow, the leaves are dark green but when dormant in hot sun, they turn a rich purple-red. This species prefers diffuse sun and will offset freely.

△ SIDE VIEW

Tightly packed, scale-like leaves curve in towards the stem tip

△ VIEW FROM ABOVE

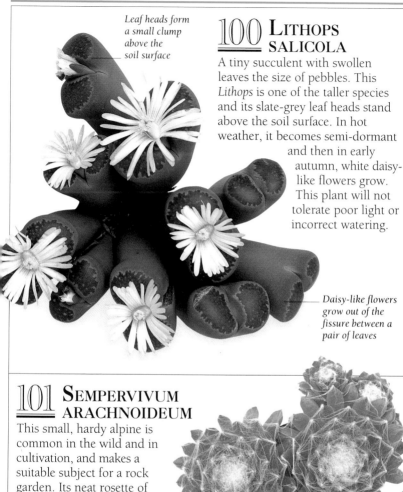

Leaf heads form a small clump above the soil surface

100 LITHOPS SALICOLA

A tiny succulent with swollen leaves the size of pebbles. This *Lithops* is one of the taller species and its slate-grey leaf heads stand above the soil surface. In hot weather, it becomes semi-dormant and then in early autumn, white daisy-like flowers grow. This plant will not tolerate poor light or incorrect watering.

Daisy-like flowers grow out of the fissure between a pair of leaves

101 SEMPERVIVUM ARACHNOIDEUM

This small, hardy alpine is common in the wild and in cultivation, and makes a suitable subject for a rock garden. Its neat rosette of leaves offsets freely in spring to form a spreading carpet of foliage. In summer, the rosettes of this *Sempervivum* species are covered in a "cobweb" of filaments.

INDEX

ACKNOWLEDGMENTS

Dorling Kindersley would like to thank Hilary Bird for compiling the index, Lesley Malkin for proof-reading, and Robert Campbell for page make-up assistance.

Photography
KEY: t *top*; b *bottom*; c *centre*; l *left*; r *right*
All photographs by Peter Anderson and Steve Gorton except for:
Linda Burgess 39; Geoff Dann 8, 9cr; Jeff Foot 10b; John Glover 19tr; Dave King 14, 15cl, 16, 17cl, 17bl, 18, 20tr, 21tl, 21b, 22, 28br; Jorge Provenza 10tr; Juliette Wade 2; Mathew Ward 15br, 25br, 26b, 27tl, 29, 31, 40br, 44bl, 45tr, 45br, 52b.

Illustrations
Andrew Farmer